Chocolate Verselets

POEMS BY PRISCILLA

PRISCILLA MULENGA CAMPBELL

authorHOUSE®

AuthorHouse™ UK
1663 Liberty Drive
Bloomington, IN 47403 USA
www.authorhouse.co.uk
Phone: 0800 047 8203 (Domestic TFN)
+44 1908 723714 (International)

Published by AuthorHouse 07/04/2019

ISBN: 978-1-7283-8020-9 (sc)
ISBN: 978-1-7283-8021-6 (hc)
ISBN: 978-1-7283-8022-3 (e)

Print information available on the last page.

This book is printed on acid-free paper.

To my parents, Stanley and Delphine Mulenga.

Acknowledgement

I would like to acknowledge my brother, Andrew Mulenga for his unfailing support from the very beginning. For approving my first poem, for his guidance and constant proof-reading.

Thanks to my husband, James, for his love, support and tedious proof-reading.

My children, Chileshe and John-Paul for putting up with me during the process.

My friends, Guiseppe, Yassin, Alina and Mwamba for their encouragement, thoughts and ideas.

Introduction

Chocolate verselets is an anthology of poems that are inspired by real life events as well as the author's resourceful imagination. Because of the ostensibly intuitive and personal nature of these poems, the author does not follow any poetic school of thought or adhere to any poetic or literary narrative other than that of her own. This is not to say she ignores any form of metrical rhythm.

In turn, this element adds a sense of innocence and transparency that may appeal to many readers. Within the pages of this book, the reader will find healthy dosages of unfulfillable longing, joy, pain, sorrow, happiness and above all, love.

All these elements add to the sweetness of life, sweetness akin to that of chocolate, administered in minute verses; verselets, Chocolate Verselets.

My Heart

My heart beats for you and only you.
My soul yearns for your soul and only yours.
My being dances to the music of you and only you.
Fine-tuned to the beat of you,
You play me a love song.
Our song.
Our love song.
No matter where I am, I catch your vibrations
Calling me,
Needing me,
Searching for me.
For my heart has a void space only you can fill.
In my world, you are the man I need.
You are my world.
No one else will do.
No one else can do.
My heart is utterly and totally devoted to you.
The music of your soul rocks my entire universe.
The void in my heart will wait for you,
And only you.
For it beats and yearns for you and only you.

Let's Play Nature

If you were a flower,
I would count the petals.
If even, then I would know you loved me not.
If odd, then for sure you do.
If you were a flower, you would have the sweetest nectar.
And I a bee,
I would collect the nectar and keep it in a jug for keeps.
If you were a bird and I the feathers,
I would ask God to use super glue to stick us tighter.
If you were a rat and I the queen of cats,
I would pass a law against rat eating
To save you for myself.
If you were harmless bacteria,
A rare species of course,
I would culture you and
Then preserve you through the years.
If you were a tree on a hilltop
And I a tree at the foot of the hill,
I would search for your roots till they joined mine.
My love for you is as natural as ocean waves,
As ancient as the tides that hit the rock at sea.
I love you; oh, yes, I do.
Though I believe not in fairy tales,
What a paradox it all is!
If a wish was to be granted unto me,
I would wish we would be together forever and ever.

Last Love Song

I have sung many a love song.
Many a love song I have sung.
This is my last, my last love song this shall be.
I know because I know, because I know.
I just know it.
It's the loudest I've sung.
The most overwhelming of all.
The most consuming,
The most compelling.
One I have no control of, charmed by the
whim of the other player of the song.
Not the deepest I've dived,
Yet the strongest vibrations I've felt … ever.
His eyes a mirror,
A reflection of what I feel.
How can this be?
His eyes deep pools of emotion,
Killing me,
Killing me ever so softly,
Ever so gently.
Silently, sensually, our souls sing a love song to each other.
Our love song,
The loudest I've ever sung.
Like waves of forever, my soul is caught up.
Ripples to the very core of me.
Alas, my soul is weary and tired, tired of singing love songs

For it has sung many a love song.
Don't want to sing anymore.
Alas, it's the loudest I've ever sung,
The strongest I've been moved,
And yet the one I cannot quite have.
I have sung many a love song.
Many a love song I have sung.
This is my last; my last love song this shall be.
I know because I know, because I know.

My Love from the Foot of Mount Etna

Unannounced, you walked into my life
Like no other.
The moment I laid my eyes on you, I loved you.
Catching me unawares.
I was mystified by your charm.
For like no other, you take my breath away.
You own my soul.
I love you; I adore you, I need you.
I am a slave to your command.
Incomplete I feel when you're not with me.
I have an illness only you can cure.
My love, my sweet, sweet love,
I want you in my life forever.
My love, my sweet, sweet love,
You are the remedy I need.
My crush, my Sicilian love,
My soul pines for your love.
My baby, my sweet, sweet baby,
You are my heart's desire
For like no other, you own my heart.
Like no other, you complete my being.
Like no other, you walked into my life and
made me realise Who I really was.
I love you; oh, yes I do, my Catanian love.

Missing You

When I need you
And I miss you,
I close my eyes, and I feel you.
Strong enough to light the Eiffel Tower,
The emotion I feel for you.
So strong it can drive a train on the London Underground.
Like the Northern Lights,
My love for you can light up the sky.
You are the desire of my whole being.
You align me.
You fix me.
You bring me to life.
When I miss you and I'm needy of you,
I close my eyes, and I can feel your heartbeat.
I feel your essence.
I feel you from afar, across the distance.
When I miss you and I'm needy of you, I
just close my Eyes, and I'm with you.

Closed Door

I had a feeling.
A feeling I did have.
Last week
I walked away, not wanting anymore.
I moved on.
I moved on, oh, yes, I did!
I shut it, and I did not want to open it,
Regretting ever meeting you.
I regretted you,
Regretted us,
Regretted whatever we shared.
I closed the door, and I locked it,
Putting the memory of you away
Carefully, tenderly, ever so gently.
Never to open it again.
Alas,
I went back to have a look-see.
Your gravity pulling me back, I stood no chance.
I could not ride the wave of chance.
See, see where it dropped me?
On some random randomness,
A random shore of forever.
Last week I shut the door.
I shut the door on us.
Alas, I went and had a look-see.
The gravity of you, the gravity of you.

Talk to Me

Tell me you love me.
Say it to me again; I need to hear it once more.
Say it to me and mean it; mean it with all your heart.
Mean it from the bottom of your heart.
Mean it from the middle of your heart.
Mean it from the top of your heart.
Mean it from the bottom to the middle
to the top of your heart.
Tell me you love me, and I will be yours now and forever.
Let me show you how much I love you.
Let me tell you what you mean to me.
I want to hear it once more from you.
Yes, tell me you love me because you
mean the universe to me.

Show Me the Path

Buried beneath the deep sea
or at the end of the rainbow,
Lead me.
Show me how to reach it.
On the summit of the sun?
Or embedded between the millions of stars in the galaxy?
The path that leads to where your love lies
I long to find
For how long must I wait for you?
How long till you reveal where your love lies?
Whatever stands in the way,
Determined I am to remove till I find your love.
For nothing would keep me from finding you.
Not the heat of the Sahara
Nor the cold of Antarctica.
Will I have to take a chance to catch it
like the aurora of the north?
I would travel across the seven seas to reach your love.
Traverse barren terrain
Just to reach that place,
The place where your love lies.

For how long must I wait for you to reveal yourself to me?
Must I wait millennia?
I long to belong to you.
I long to hear your song.
I long to hear the song that will reveal
where you have placed your love.
I long to find your song that will lead me to your heart.
For I long to find the path that will lead
me to where your Love is hidden.

A Part of Me

I will always carry you where you belong:
In my heart.
I will always think of you—
Every day.
You blow my mind.
I will never forget you
For as long as I live.
I will care for you always.

Forever

If I wait for you,
Would you come looking for me?
If you told me
That you miss me,
I would come to you.
Do you think of me?
Always?
Sometimes?
Never?
Would you?
Oh … would you?
Would you keep yourself for me?
If you asked me to keep myself for you,
My darling, I would.

Fruity Love

I pluck you a lemon
from my orchard of love.
I make a glass of sweet, cool lemonade
For my beau.

I pluck an apple.
I carve it into the apple of my eye
For you are the apple of my eye.

I then pluck you a melon.
Its freshness
Will refresh your soul.

For I have tried to hate you.
Alas, all is in vain.
No point in trying anymore.

I try to run away from you.
Alas, your soul calls for mine
So loudly the eardrums of my heart never stop.

I pluck you a red berry,
The colour of love.

I stroll slowly, silently
In the garden of forever.
Your face is all I see.

I pluck you a fruit, a sign of well-being.
I pick you a rose,
A red rose.
My heart lays it at your feet.
I pluck you a red rose.
I lay it at your feet.
I wash your feet
With the oil I make in my heart
For you.

I pluck a fruit for you.
I pluck a rose for you.
For my heart is an oasis, harbouring all this love for you.

Guilty Pleasure

My darling, my sweet darling,
To me, you are the very air I breathe.
My sweetie, my sweetest sweet,
I desire your lips like drops of honey.
My love, my dearest love,
To hold you is like heaven to me.
My gorgeous, my forever gorgeousness,
Your essence fills my presence.
For how can I get away from you
When you fill my senses?
You are the component of the air that keeps me vibrant.
From the moment I set my eyes on you,
I have needed you
Gnawing at my soul.
You take over my whole being,
Never to be the same again.
I'm in constant need of you.
A dose of you, I need you close.
My pleasure, my guilty pleasure,
The pleasure of having you is bittersweet
For in my mind I have left you so many times,
Yet my heart cannot let you go.

My baby, my precious baby,
Come closer; let me care for you.
My angel, my perfect angel, how I long to be held by you.
My darling, my sweet darling, I'm living
for the day I shall behold you next.

The Man in My Dream

He seduced my soul, and I loved it.
Feeling at home,
Knowing he was the one I was waiting for,
For the barrier had lifted.
The floodgates had opened,
And my spirit was singing within the very depth of me.
I try to shut those gates.
Alas, the current is too strong; it has
broken them—cannot be mended.
And now I stand here, not knowing what to do.
I do wonder about the significance of it all
From the very beginning, he was a match not,
I wrestle,
I reason,
I reckon,
I ponder,
I wonder
For the logic in my mind agrees not.
But my heart, in a different place,
A place of peace.
A place of sincerity.

A place of love
For I feel deeply for this man.
A paradox,
I yearn for him.
He rocks my world.
He brings me home.
He is like the one I saw in my dreams,
His demeanour,
His inner man.
He is gentle.
He is kind.
He knows how to hold me when he holds me.
I don't want him to go away, ever.
How can this be?

Horses

If wishes were horses,
I would ride the very first as it passes by.
If I could reach out and catch my lucky star to have you,
I would.
If I had to sail the seven seas,
Traverse the Sahara
By plane or sail
For you, I would.
If I could dream and make it reality,
The reality would be you and me.

Innocence

His name is Innocence
For a pure soul he had,
As pure as a ray of light.
He made the night alight
For he lit my fire.

I could feel his essence
For he had nothing to hide.
His face glowed with innocence and purity.
His eyes a sea of tranquillity.

I fell for it.
Alas, I fell hard,
Falling as helpless as a leaf
For my soul was alight by this man of innocence.

Not able to contain me,
The strength of it pushed him away.
If only it could be undone,
I would do just that.

As gentle as a dove,
As delicate as a child,
His touch serene.
His whole-body vibrating beauty,
A beauty untapped, untouched,
To be violated not.

His nakedness a sea of ecstasy,
Like velvet to my touch.
The man I met with a pure heart brushed my very soul.
Alas, he was mine not.
For if he was, he would take me as I am.

So, I cast him upon the waters,
Where his soul longs to be,
Hoping that someone finds him and loves him as he is.
But I forget him not,
And his footsteps shall remain
on the sandy beach of the sea in my heart.

The Promise

I made a promise.
A promise I made.
Promised to love you till I die.
Till I die, I promised to love you.
I promised to take care of you.
Till I die, I promised to take care of you.
A promise.
A promise.
For what is a promise?
A word? A whisper?
A sentiment? A statement?
As delicate as a butterfly's wings,
Can be broken on a whim.
Strong, yet fragile.
You mean it.
You keep it.
You break it.
Yet, in a way, everlasting.
I made a promise, a promise I made.
Till death do we part.
Quite a statement, don't you think?
Till I die, till I die, to have, and to hold.
I will love you till the day I die.

Drift Away

Every night as I put my head on my pillow,
My thoughts carry me away.
I meet my fantasy,
My man,
My heartthrob.
O I wish I could see him right now
For I miss talking with him,
Being with him.
Goodnight, my fantasy lover.
Goodnight.

Juliet

The heat, the heat,
I feel the heat.
Explosions,
Explosions, I see them in the sky.
Emotions, sensations,
Raw emotion from you to me, from me to you.
Honey,
Drops of honey,
Floods of milk and honey.
Oh … so sweet, so pure, so true.
A whisper, a whimper,
A moan, a groan.
Your heartbeat, my heartbeat
Synchronised
For just a moment yet impacting on me forever.
Your eyes, shining bright,
So bright they illuminate the room,
Illuminating my soul.
How can this be?
How can I find such purity in the forbidden?
You are my Romeo,
My hero, my fantasy lover.
You are real; in my world, just you and me.
My heart beating for you and only you.

My breath you have taken.
My heart you have stolen.
My very being an envelope full of emotion for you.
My Romeo, my Romeo, I am indeed your Juliet.

Message in a Bottle

I send you a message,
A little message of hope,
A message in a bottle.
I cast it upon the sea, hoping it gets to you.
If I could,
I would carry it across to you.
Trek the harsh desert like an Arab man just to see you
For you know I would walk a thousand
miles if I could only see you.
I send you a message—
Hope it does get to you—
Of peace and love,
Saying that the Almighty is watching over you,
Taking care of your needs.
For you need not worry; only trust in Him.
A message from my heart.
I would cross the seven seas to get to where you are,
To see your smile,
To hear your voice.
I send a message in a bottle to you,
Sealing it very tight lest it gets destroyed.
For it's a message from deep within,
A message from my heart, flowing with love,
Just to tell you,
To tell you that you tickle my soul.
To tell you I cannot sleep.

I can barely eat.
I lie wake at night;
I toss,
I turn.
To tell you that I wonder.
I wonder why
I dream of you
Even though our paths met but then
they parted for some reason,
Reasons only our God knows.
That's why I send you this message,
This message in a bottle.
A message I cast upon the waters, hoping it gets to you.
A message to say my heart is indeed full of you.
A message that must get to you whether
I see you again or not.

My Guy

My guy is the best.
To the East and to the West, he is still the best.
Go down South, he will still be the best.
Check the Arctic; no one would compare to him.
He holds me close.
He holds me tight.
I feel it inside.
He holds my hand.
I nearly go wild.
I see in his eyes he loves me too.
I'd rather have him than a million dollars.
I'd rather go poor than not have him to love.
I'd rather sit by his side and tell him
just how much I love him.
My guy's the best.
He sings love songs to me.
He is by my side when I need him most.
He will never go away.
I have found my guy.
I have found my guy
I have found true happiness.
I have found true love in my guy
For my guy is simply the best.

My Love

Like a ring,
My love for you is
With no end; my love for you is,
It is sincere.
I love you for you.
I love what you see in the mirror each
day when you wake up,
And that's the person I will always love
For my love is endless,
As endless as a ring.

Catania

I had an encounter with a man.
A brief encounter it was for it lasted only a moment.
It had to last a moment;
It could not last more than that moment.
It ended before it could even begin.
So, I say goodbye.
Goodbye to the man who captured
my heart for but a moment.
For how does one make a moment last forever?
I longed for that moment to last forever.
I longed for a kiss.
His kiss.
Just one kiss.
In that kiss, I could've felt his essence,
His being, his beauty, his soul.
I've dreamed of his kiss.
In my dreams, I've felt this kiss,
The kiss of a moment that would last forever.
I say goodbye.
Crawling back into my shell, I cast the moment upon the
Waters to be carried away,
Carried away to a place where the moment will last forever.
In another land, another world, another lifetime.
In that lifetime, that moment is reality.

I say goodbye to the man who, by his look,
made my whole being excited.
For his eyes made me feel like a beautiful woman.
His eyes told me he wanted me as I am.
His eyes told me he desired me.
The man who made me feel emotions I never knew existed.
For my whole essence was alive and could feel,
Yet this moment was never mine to have.
So, I say goodbye.
Goodbye, my crush from Catania

Over My Shoulder

Every now and again, I look over my shoulder.
Every now and again, I wonder if I will see you there.
Every now and again, I wonder if you
are there, waiting for me.
For I wonder if you think of me ... ever.
I wonder why it all had to happen.
I secretly miss you ... still.
I secretly hope you will be there over
my shoulder when I look,
Waiting, wanting, missing.
Secretly I wish you would come looking.
Silently, I hear myself whisper your name.
A whisper, a whimper, a moan, a groan.
For every now and again, I whisper your name to myself,
Hoping you hear me.
I reach out to you.
Secretly, I hope you are needy of me too.
"I miss you."
Words that go on and on in my head,
On and on, like waves from my radio.
Words I'm tired of hearing on the radio.

Every now and again, you come to me in my thoughts.
Every now and again, I see you in my dreams.
Every now and again, someone mentions your name.
I look over my shoulder, hoping you will appear.
I secretly expect you to come back one day
For goodbye are words I secretly never wanted to say …
"I miss you."

Amsterdam

I found a gem,
But I cannot have it.
It's on the top shelf;
I'm vertically challenged.
On tiptoe I cannot reach
The top shelf; there the gem is—
A precious stone.
I found it, yet I cannot reach it; therefore, I cannot keep it.
I grab a stool, I lean forward,
I tiptoe, I tiptoe,
I express myself.
The gem moves away slowly.
Ever so slowly, ever so gently.
Why do I feel this gem is a key to my happiness
When clearly it is not?
Could it be the key to my happiness?
Or is it an illusion, a false promise,
A vision?
A vision of love, I reach out to touch; it's
beyond my reach, I cannot quite grasp.
Ever so slowly, it edges away from me.
So, I tiptoe, I tiptoe.
Farther away it moves.
I found a gem on the top shelf.

A stone more precious
I doubt I've ever seen.
I reach out to touch it
For I need to have it.
I cannot have it; I cannot have it.
You are to me my precious stone, yet I cannot have you.

Volcano

What do you do?
What do you do with an erupted volcano?
Let the lava flow, destroying all that crosses its path.
It burns anything that dares impede its path.
What do you do with an erupted volcano?
What do you do with emotions awakened?
It is irreversible.
It cannot be put to sleep again
For feelings cannot be unfelt.
Things cannot go back to how they were.
Things just cannot be the same.
Suddenly, the beauty in your eyes is no more.
Suddenly, I do not feel you.
Suddenly, your eyes do not transport me to euphoria.
Suddenly, your eyes do not make me
feel like a beautiful woman.
Something happened.
A light was turned off
I know nothing of.
Your essence has escaped me.
Alas, I stand here with lava erupting
from my volcano for you.

Who dares stop it?
How did you stop it?
How do you stop a volcano erupting after
it's been stirred from slumber?
How do you capture emotions and put them
back into the bottle they came from?
It would be like uncrying a tear or unspeaking a word.
Alas, alas, this can be done not.
I shall sit here with the burning lava and feel,
Till this wave of emotion passes me by, burning all it
meets, yet later bringing forth a new beginning.
I will sit away.

On the Shelf

Don't leave me just like that.
Don't leave me on the shelf.
Don't put me back where you found me.
I could not bear the pain.
Where would I find another you?
Where would I find another loving soul like you?
And the memories would kill my soul.
Please understand,
Understand I will always need you
For the thought of losing you kills me.
Where would I find another you?
Please come closer.
Come closer and hold my hand.
I might feel a lot better.
Doesn't feel good when you sit that far;
Come closer.
Just this once, please come closer.
I need you closer.
Come closer.
Don't leave me on the shelf.
I need to express the sorrow that would befall me if you left.

All That Glitters

If you held out your hand to me,
Naturally, I would reach out and hold you.
When you feel lonely and lonesome,
You know I'm a call away.
For when you search to find a soul mate,
Sometimes all that glitters is not gold.
It's the soul that connects with yours
and just understands where you are at
That is the gold,
A treasure to last a lifetime.

Seven Endless Days

It is without beginning and is with no end,
As endless as a ring.
It goes on and on,
On and on in circles of forever.
I miss you
Like a waterless parched desert,
Waiting for the rain it so desperately needs.
The days are endless.
The days are long, and the nights cold.
I cannot feel you.
Just as the night gives birth to day in cycles of forever,
My longing for you is relentless
For the more I see you, the more I need you.
If I could capture you for me, I would
To behold you every moment of every single day.
You fill my senses like no other.
I desperately need to feel your presence,
Your essence,
Your heartbeat.
Like a sapling needs the rays from the sun,
I am needy of you.

My longing for you persists
Seven endless days.
As the night gives birth to day in cycles of forever,
I relentlessly long for your presence.
Till I behold you again, my days are long,
and my nights go on forever.
I miss you.

Paradox 2018

My soul perceived yours.
Your soul brushed mine.
My soul came alive for it has been in slumber.
You feel right.
You seem right.
Yet you cannot be right.
You do not belong to me.
You never have been.
You never will.
Yet I need you.
Like a drug, I pine for you.
I feel hooked.
Alas, how can this be?
Mine you shall never be,
And I, never to be yours.
Yet in my dreams, I'm yours, and you are mine.
In my dreams you hold me, and you never let me go.
In my mind we are.
I hold you as long as I desire.
In my dreams, I am yours, and you are mine—
My crush, my drug, my aphrodisiac, my desire—
For you mesmerise and consume me completely.
Your soul brushed mine.
My soul is needy of you.
Alas, how can this be?
A stranger you are to me.
A stranger whom I have known for a lifetime in my dreams.

Never Mine at All

No matter how hard I cry,
You are gone forever.
If I went out on a search hunt,
You are no more.
High and low, round and round I go; alas, all in vain.
I may mourn your death for the rest of my life.
It will do me no good
For there is no good in the whole situation.
I sometimes wish I could come to where you are,
But that I cannot do.
Whatever I say or do will not bring you back to me.
A status quo I must get used to
For I have to go on without you.
All alone I am.
How lonesome I feel.
How lonely I feel.
My feelings are nothing but my state of mind,
don't matter then, or do they?
The pain of this great loss is hard to bear.
"Time will heal," they say.
But I feel it's the kind that lasts and lasts.
For no matter how hard I cry,
You were never mine at all.

Love

The love I see around is like a fresh rose,
So beautiful in its blossom.
Colourful, as bright as a rainbow,
Promising, oh yes, to last always.
Alas, always is not forever!
I know of a love that lasts,
Never shining, hidden,
Never blooming for it's just there,
Like a pearl of an oyster
In all its beauty and splendour.
Hidden, only to be uncovered by that special someone,
If there is that special someone.
I still hold that love for you,
Never letting go for it has been cultured
and nurtured in all secrecy,
Away from all pollution.
Never will it glitter for all that glitters indeed is not gold.
If cannot, and I shall not force it,
Finding comfort in who I am.
Never will I rise to the expectations of others.
The beauty of real love lies within the heart and the soul
And is everlasting.

For love is indeed eternal.
Love is beauty,
And real beauty is love,
A beauty that grows richer and richer by the day.
A beauty that does not glitter for all to see.
A beauty from deep within that can stand the test of time.

Lie to Me

They say the truth hurts.
Well, I say the truth kills.
It gnaws at the very core of me.
Please don't tell me.
Please don't inform me.
I crave not the power that lies in knowledge.
I cannot cope with it.
I will not cope with it.
I cannot cope with the truth from you.
I repudiate your truth.
Please leave me in the not know
For the not know is cosy and bliss.
Please let me stay with the ignorant.
I find happiness there.
The truth … please don't voice it.
The truth … let me not be aware of it
For the truth, it is killing me.
I have not the capacity to contain it, so please lie to me.
The truth from you, my heart cannot
contain my ignorance is bliss.
They say the truth hurts.
I say the truth has the capacity to kill
For I died when I learned of your truth.
I died just a little bit when you decided to tell
me what you did when you went away.

If I Could

If I could, I would turn you inside out.
If I could, I would dissect your heart,
Know what's inside you.
If given a chance, I would turn you into a grand laboratory,
Study the mechanism of you.
If I could, oh yes, I would.
I would like to trap you in a glass bottle for keeps,
Or investigate you under the electronic microscope.
For I know I cannot change you; how
I wish I could just understand.
I long to understand the humanity of you.
If I could, I tell you, I would.
Your line of thought, I can comprehend not.
A complex maze it is to me.
My mind, in all its simplicity, cannot perceive.
If I could, I would, but I can't, so I will not.
I just will not try anymore.
I will love you and leave you and carry on my journey.
For understanding you, I have
discovered, was not meant to be.

Not Gold

Precipitations of love have formed in the intrinsic
Chambers of my heart.
Collecting into droplets,
They trickle down the path heading
to your heart.
With no way of stopping them, they are
Like a brakeless train on a train track,
Rolling downhill.
For a barrier I cannot erect
Lest they collect and I drown.
Thoughts of you resurface now and again
As I go about my business.
I look not at the past.
It is gone, just like seasons come and go.
I let it flow, and I let it go.
I stand at the crack of dawn,
And I welcome the sunshine into my life.
Patiently I await the future,
Allowing God's promise unto me.
I therefore allow God's gift to catch up with me
And consume me in total ecstasy,
Total bliss,
A beautiful, meaningful, deep connection.
A love so true.

For if you held out your hand to me,
Naturally, I would reach out and hold you.
And when you feel lonely and lonesome,
You know I'm a call away.
I know you search to find a soul mate.
Sometimes all that glitters is not gold.
Take a good look at me.
There is more to me than what meets the eye.
It's the soul that connects with yours
And just understands where you are at
That is the gold.
A treasure to last a lifetime.
So effortlessly, lazily,
My droplets of love are growing into pockets of love.
There is no way to stop them from growing,
So, I let them be.

Between Me and Him

Like the old times,
He held me with his eyes.
Every time I looked into those eyes,
He mesmerised me with his charm.
Oh, how will I break away from his spell?
Or do I want to, really?
Like the old times,
He walked me down the street,
Never wanting the walk to come to an end—
Was like a dream of yesterday.
Like the old times,
I felt his soul deep within me,
Locked up with each other.
Forgetting the past, beholding not the future
But experiencing the beauty of the now.
I constantly feel his conscience merge with mine.
I understand not, but I feel his strong
vibrations reach out for me.
And mine for him.
For like the old times, his eyes told me a thousand
times what could not be put into words.

Familiar but Strange

Have you ever felt the past and the present merge?
That what you are experiencing once was?
Like a form of déjà vu,
There is something very familiar about you.
You remind me of the past that once was.
I feel you within me.
I feel your emotions in me, and they feel so familiar.
I feel I have known you from another life,
In another life and dimension.
I just cannot put my finger to it.
I feel I have known you for a long time
Or existed in a coexistence,
Way back in the past.
Or is it back to the future?
Feeling at home in your presence,
It's like a home away from home.
You are familiar,
A familiar stranger.
But your familiarity is strange,
And I do not want to have anything to do with it.

Emotions on the Move

On the move, my emotions
Constantly
Bombard the walls of my heart.
It's a game I play, and I hate to play,
Leaving me helpless, worked out, yearning.
Oh, a much-needed break.
Futile are my efforts to put an end to it.
Watch out, lest you catch it.
For it's like an epidemic,
Catches you unawares,
Leaving you overwhelmed as if carrying
the world on your shoulders.
Like tides smashing against rock strata,
Constantly my emotions go round and round.
Like a never-ending story,
I stare at your photo.
Feeling helpless, you insist on staying on my mind.
You look real.
Can almost touch you, can almost smell
you, can almost hear your voice.
I stare at your photo,
So helpless,
Helplessly in love with you.

My emotions are on the move constantly,
Bombarding against the walls of my heart
With no way of getting out.
It's a game I must play for as long as it takes.

Sorry

With the effortlessness of the autumn leaf,
The pull of gravity upon its centre,
Forgive me, I fell for you.
Your pull towards me,
Like gravity upon that leaf,
I could not resist.
I am sorry
I took the liberty,
The liberty to fall for you
As effortless as a raindrop,
Or as effortlessly as morning dew,
Falling freely, loosely, covering all exposed objects.
Silently, gently, softly,
The pull of you,
The pull of you.
For how can I defy gravity?
Like the very breath I take,
I dare not flout nature.
I dare not swim against the current.
Forgive me, I took the liberty to follow my heart,
To be free.
To live.
To feel.

Like the autumn leaf, choice is not an option.
It has to fall.
I'm sorry I could not stop it.
I'm sorry I let it happen, yet it was effortless.
I'm sorry I fell, and you were not there to catch me as I fell.

Sudden Change

Why did you call?
Why did you pick up the phone and give me a buzz?
Doing more harm than good, you said you would change.
All in vain.
I felt so down,
So depressed,
So low.
Worse than before, I drown in my sorrow.
For my emotions were under control.
My feelings,
My mind,
My body,
My soul.
You came in and disturbed the status quo,
Distorting my peace of mind; I've lost
the peace of mind I once enjoyed.
Awakening a sudden civil war within
the chambers of my heart,
Or the curiosity of a boy poking at a beehive.
For I had my emotions locked up in a tight vessel
Under strict inspection,
Under systematic control.

But there you went,
Tampering with my sore spot; now it hurts
Oh, ever so much.
Why did you call?
For indeed your absence felt far warmer
than the presence you bring unto me.

Sunshine

The essence of you disappeared
Like quicksand.
You slipped through my fingers.
I held you, yet I did not catch you.
I beheld you, yet I did not have you.
My glow is diminishing.
I am losing the fire you lit.
My sunshine gone, I feel the sunset coming upon me.
You are not here.
You are not here.
You illuminated my being, giving me the ability to feel.
But you are gone.
I've lost my essence and my feeling;
I cannot feel life Anymore.
Your essence brings me life.
Your essence brings me feeling.
Your essence brings me meaning.
Your essence brings me hope.
With the setting sun, the night draws in.
I behold the strong, bright rays of the
setting sun piercing my soul,
Teasing, taunting, mocking,
Bidding me farewell.

You are not here.
You are not here.
And I am losing all sense of feeling.
With the essence of you disappeared, I feel the
sunshine No more, and the winter is nigh.

The Essence of Our Affair

Tell me the meaning of it all.
What is the essence of our affair?
To say you are not serious tears me apart
For I ask for not much more than your love,
A love taking me as I am.
A love that will tell right from wrong.
A love sincere in all aspects.
Please be afraid not.
I wish you good will and love,
Happiness and joy
With the innocence of a child,
A purity of fresh, running water.
My love for you is true.
All I ask is for your love in return
Through the winter,
Through the summer,
Through all seasons.
My love for you will last
For that!
That is the very essence of this affair.

Fantasy

Like a fantasy, it never was.
Built on a rock that would wear away,
Like a castle in the sky,
Subject to nature's pull.
A bed of roses I thought it would be.
Unrealistic he was.
Acts of love,
Acting out his love for me,
Wanting to please where one cannot.
A dream that cannot be lived
For we both thought we would never go wrong.
The perfect couple.
Now I see the light.
I see how childlike it all was.
Our love was based on things that would fade away.
For you, I feel something different.
For you, I have a feeling that just understands.
For you, I accept anything that comes my way.
Tomorrow may take you away from me.
I feel beauty
Cannot be ruined by anyone or anything.

The beauty that makes me feel and accept who you are
run deep within me.
Yes, a feeling with no attachments.
Never wanting to cling to you, should you wish to move on.
A feeling that will always be strong for you
Whether you feel the same or not.

Without Him

My heart breaks.
My heart breaks, alas.
I never had him for how can a heart
break for a man I never had?
The sadness deep within my soul
immense, inconsolable, dramatic.
Nothing can soothe.
The fire you lit, nothing can quench.
For I miss you.
I love you.
I long for your gentle touch,
And I am needy for you.
Yet you never belonged to me
And never will.
O why can I not move on and get over you?
Move on and shut the door behind me.
Keeping me hostage, your essence and
beauty have captivated me.
I cannot be free.
My heart breaks.
My soul bleeds.
My body pines for the touch of your
hands on my bare skin.

With each passing day,
the sadness within my soul deepens.
For my heart breaks for a man who never belonged to me.
Now, here I am.
I stand alone,
Unable to unfeel what only he made me feel.
Learning to live without him, alas,
I have lived with him Not!
Remnants of his flavour remain within
me, yet I have tasted him not!
My heart breaks, and my soul bleeds.
A feeling I'm too familiar with.
A feeling I dread yet embrace for I miss my
crush from the foot of Mount Etna.

Pastures Anew

Looking from over here,
Pastures always look greener and lush,
The deception of the mirage.
It seems beautiful, perfectly romantic, and true.
It seems blissful, delightful,
Captivating my soul,
Taking my breath away.
I lost control.
Alas, pastures are never greener,
Never better,
Never different.
I stand here in absolute confusion,
Knowing what to do a sheer luxury.
The old pasture seems too dead.
Revival a tedious expedition.
The new pasture, mirage, I cannot quite grasp.
So, I sit away.
Alone, no one to relate to.
Can anyone hear me?
Hello, is there someone out there?
Wandering in no man's land, searching for the answers.
When will this end?
For the pastures anew were not greener, and
the present pastures close to no more.
I therefore balance in an abyss,
Hoping I shall land on a pasture I will finally call home.

Walls and Fences

All around me I see them
To protect,
To keep in,
To keep out,
To preserve, to conserve
Walls and fences, walls and fences.
Walls of justice,
Walls of injustice,
Walls that separate,
Walls that keep us close.
Breaking them down, an injustice in itself.
No one dares.
I've seen them all my life.
I've lived them all my life.
For I've lived in a wall of self for years.
Policies, politics, schools, religion,
Race, greed, culture.
Walls that allow the essence of belonging.
Walls that include, walls that exclude,
Perceiving them each and every day.
One cannot help but wonder and ponder.
Walls and fences, walls and fences.
We've done a good job
Excluding the included,
Breaking down walls and fences of exclusion,
Yet rebuilding walls of inclusion.

Silent Place

I know of a place,
A place where nothing moves.
A place where nothing talks.
It's a peaceful place.
No one can reach it;
It's too far away.
Many people start out to reach it.
They start hoping to find it,
But all in vain.
I have been there, to the silent place,
But I had to come back.
I was sent back,
Back to this place,
This place full of noise, misunderstanding,
Hunger, poverty, greed, hatred, and dishonesty.
I still live for the day I will go back,
Back to the silent place,
Knowing it's still there; it will always be.
For it is as still as the wind on a hot day.
Time never passes.
I know of a place.
I know of a silent place,
A place deep within me,
A place I can call home.

Maybe

Maybe, just maybe,
This is all I need.
Maybe I was expecting too much,
Maybe much, but not too much to ask for.
Maybe care and love are indeed enough.
Maybe there is happiness to be found in all this.
Maybe his love language is different from mine.
Maybe I need to learn his.
Maybe he needs to learn mine.
Maybe I do have everything I need.
Maybe I am led to pastures anew, pastures green.
Maybe my soul is renewed each day.
Maybe the grand plan is different to my understanding.
Maybe, just maybe, this is indeed all I need.
The simplicity, the calmness.
The honesty, pure love from the heart.
Maybe I need not go looking.
Maybe what I seek is right here with me.
Maybe in the stillness of his nature my happiness lies.
Maybe, just maybe, I could be happy,
For maybe all I seek is right before my very eyes.

The Rope

The first thought I have in the morning,
The very first feeling I experience,
Is the thought that you are no more.
Though I have known this for some time now,
The reality of each day
Always a shock to me, the reality that you are gone is real.
I remained hanging by the rope.
The rope that you had let go of.
You did that way before you finally said goodbye.
I kept on, hoping that things would be right.
Hopeless feelings called love, my hope was based on.
The love that ceased before your time to go.
I could not figure that one out till the end.
And now I remain alone for a love that was not to be.
How I wish you could tell me.
How I wish you could tell me what I needed to know,
For I was waiting for you to do so.
Now it's too late.
Time was on your side, not.
And so, you left me hanging by the rope.
The rope you had let go of
Way before I could realise.
The feeling I have each morning is the shock
that I will not see your face again.

The Little African

Gentle, kind, giving, and true,
I once visited little Marrakech.
True friend,
Loyal like a solider, supports you like a brother.
I found the little African a source of strength.
My adviser,
My friend,
My confidant.
With vibrant colours,
Little Marrakech shines.
Planner and executer,
Intelligence,
Hustler, fighter,
Yet a believer in his God.
A true advocate of the faith passed on.
I once visited little Marrakech.
I found the little African living there.
I came back empowered by this encounter,
Enriched by its beauty, the purity, and his faith.
I shall always visit little Marrakech.
I shall always visit my little African friend.

Sisterhood

When I need comfort, I look across.
When I need a friend, I look across.
I only have to look across when I'm distressed,
And I see her, like a ray of sunshine kissing my skin.
I feel her warmth, her love, her exquisiteness.
My solace.
My oasis.
My sister.
Kindred spirits.
We've only just met, yet I know I've
known you from forever.
Another life, another dimension, another place.
A bag of love you are.
Sensitive yet strong,
Delicate yet agile.
A bag of love you are.
Wise beyond your years.
A pleasure,
A joy,
A delight.

When I need a friend, I look across, and there you are.
There you are,
And I know you are there.
My sister, my bag of love and affection, my confidante.
Like a ray of sunshine,
Your beauty is as warm and captivating as the sun.
Keep shining.

Pass Away

I have to learn to be alone
Now that you are gone.
I better get used to life without you.
Each passing day,
I grow further away.
However, nearer to the day I shall finally see you again.
Memories are but a shadow of yesterday.
Just as grass comes to pass away,
My love, ours came to pass away.

Roommate

Sweet and true,
Doing her own thing.
So much she has on her mind
She manages to brush aside.
Life goes on.
Life must go on.
The spirit to accept she has built inside herself.
The type who can sit and wait,
Wait for what she knows will happen to happen.
She does not express her feelings.
Locking them up, she is always cool, calm, and collected.
She is strong, the type who survives.
My roommate is sweet and kind.
She is sweet and true.
My roommate is able to stand the test of time.

Lisbon

A memory I cannot quite remember.
You remind me of a place and a moment.
You fill me with excitement; you invigorate me.
Adventurers, voyagers, conquerors,
You are but a shadow of the might you once possessed,
Yet you inspire me.
You stir within me the need to achieve,
Yet you have seen better days.
A mighty empire no more, I perceive
remnants of what once was.
You bring me comfort.
You console me; you understand me.
You seem familiar to me,
Like I've met you before.
Spectacular
Splendour.
Your soul is not there anymore; I cannot feel you.
I cannot feel you, yet you spoke to me.
You console me, yet you trigger me,
Sending me mixed vibes; I cannot settle.
You remind me of a place.
You remind me of streets I once walked,
streets I once lived.

Lisbon, you are indeed an old friend for
you are familiar yet strange.
You console, you comfort, you invigorate.
Yet you are not there.
Your very soul left, yet I perceive fragments
of the mighty empire you are no more.

I Stand Alone

In the midst of plenty, I lack.
I feel the crowd pressing on,
Yet I am alone.
I cannot truly commit to any soul.
I stand alone.
I feel alone.
In the midst of the crowd, I am lonely and lonesome,
Longing for solitude yet needing company.
A paradox indeed.
I long for solitude, company,
Having the desire to connect.
Yet my soul is too far removed to connect,
Possessing not the ability.
My soul roams into limbo,
Neither here, neither there.
With no one, I stand and feel alone.
I guess a loner I always have been.
A loner I always will be,
Sociable yet distant,
For my soul lacks the ability to truly
connect my heart to anyone.

Journey

A tear, a laugh, another tear,
Anguish, regret,
Blessings, graces from the Almighty.
My journey hard, my lesions deep,
I'm strong enough not to weep.
For I had to soldier on; it wasn't fair, but I had to bear
My journey, my path, my existence, me.
Violated, abused, misunderstood, I
stand alone on my throne.
Too soon stripped naked, all taken
away from me, I feel helpless.
I stand alone
For it is relentless.
Exhausted, emptied, drained.
My help came from no other but Him.
For what is happiness? Alas, just an emotion.
A journey that has been bittersweet.
I run, I walk, I fall, I get up.
I fight it no more.
I breathe.
I sing.
I feel.
I accept.
I breathe yet again.

Graces, joy, contentment.
A life without Him I dare not think of.
In a nutshell, here I am
As I am.
I sigh…. I breathe.

Freedom

Whatever it was that drew you to me
Brought out the best in me.
I'm ready to blossom,
Blossom and shine.
What a journey.
What an adventure.
What a dream.
New chapter,
New era,
New horizons.
I feel renewed and free,
Free to be me.
I can be me.
I have allowed myself to be seen.
The veil has been lifted.
I can let the world in.
I feel the world will let me be me.
I shall blossom.
The little girl can express herself.
There's no room for fear, tears, or regret.
I therefore embrace me and let me be seen.
No camouflage, no pretence, no disguise.
That which brought you to me permits me
to be the person I was meant to be.

Echoes

Familiar sounds—
Echoes reaching out to me, grabbing me.
The laughter of children,
Loud noises,
Quiet noises.
Echoes that vibrate, reminding me.
Laughter,
The sound of life itself.
Feet shuffling.
A wink, a whiff,
A smile,
Flowers.
Sensations—
Familiar sensations.
My past,
My present,
My future
Fused into one.
Echoes, echoes filling my very being.
Feels like I'm looking in from the outside
For I'm numb, and I'm dumb.

Echoes of the yesterday,
Vibrations of the present,
The promise—
Yes, the promise of tomorrow.
Familiar sounds, laughter,
Vibrations of life reminding me …
I reminisce, contemplate,
Why? Why am I sitting here?
What is the meaning of all this?

Dreams

You have been gone awhile now,
Yet I still see you in my dreams.
I have moved on; really, I have.
Yet, you still appear in my dreams.
What is it that you want me to feel?
You are just no more.
Makes me wonder.
There's no meaning at all in those dreams.
I have always said what I feel,
Yet what I feel is hard to explain
For you have been gone awhile.
Days have drifted away,
Making months
And months; months have bled into years.
Yet I still feel you.
But I've got to let you go
And meet someone new.
Knowing I will love you in my own special way,
I do thank God for the time I did spend with you.
But now I'm ready to meet someone new.

Dimensions

Amongst the living, I cannot live.
Amongst the dead, I cannot rest.
So, I shall live in the land of the nowhere.
You can see it not.
Yet like the rays from the sun, you can feel it.
Only to be perceived by the gentle—
The whisper—
The gentle breeze,
The silhouette.
Cannot touch it for it is fragile.
The land of the in-between,
Where my soul can rest.
The world of the living is too real,
Too intense,
Too brutal.
The dead, the dead are gone.
One cannot retrieve it or take part in it.
Cannot touch the dead as they have gone to another place.
So, I sail away to the land of the in between,
The gentle place I feel safe to dwell.

An Answer to Yesterday

If you search deep within you,
You will find a dwelling place.
The sort of place that knows no sorrow or pain.
The sort of place where one experiences
deep, complete happiness.
I feel that spot in you,
That calmness deep within you.
Though you have fear of the tomorrow,
And indeed, regrets of the yesterday,
Composed you remain still.
A composure from deep within,
I reach out to touch it.
I cannot find it,
But I know it's there
For you emote vibrations from this place.
I feel them from you.
Yesterday is gone;
Tomorrow is yet to come;
The present is all we have.
The today is lived better
Because of the experience of the yesterday
And the hope of the tomorrow.
The promise of the today is worth living
For today is better lived after a yesterday and
before the tomorrow that may never be.

He Lives in Me

You have loved me since eternity.
From the beginning of time
You have known me.
Eternally you have perceived me.
The clear concept,
A clear vision I was unto you.
I cannot hold back; you're the planner of
the life You gave me.
Your body broken, out of control.
Pretence an act so foreign.
For love from the intrinsic part of you
Is overflowing.
Cannot stop it.
I therefore lay me at your feet in humility,
My bosom a resting place for your head.
My love eternal.
My soul homeless.
My heart bleeding for you.
My mind sustained by my God.
My passion locked up within me.
For I cannot present it to yet another soul.
Your passion becoming my passion.
Happy Easter.

Pillow Talk

I put my head on my pillow.
I pray to my God.
I pray to my God to see my beau again, please.
I send him a pocket,
A pocket delivered secretly in the night.
A pocket of love.
A gentle kiss wrapped in a vesicle of love.
I say a prayer.
I count the stars.
I behold a falling star.
I make a wish.
I put up my Christmas tree.
With every decoration,
I make a wish,
I say a prayer,
I make a wish
For my heart bleeds for him.
I sent him a kiss as I put my head on my pillow,
Delivered to the doorstep of his heart,
To caress him gently.
My soul longs for him.
Seems like eternity since I last saw him.
My thoughts of him so numerous in a day.

I virtually live with him in my heart.
So real.
So real I say, "Good morning," and, "Goodnight," each day.
I rest my head on my pillow at night.
I pray to God that "I may see you again, please,
For you are my heart's desire.
Like a glove on a hand, you are the man who fits my soul,
And you are the man I truly want."

Clusters of Love

Bubbles of love erupting from deep within,
Like a volcano—erupting!
Alas, I can stop them not!
Butterflies in my tummy.
Oh, dear, what will I do with me?
I once had footprints on the sand,
of the shores, of the seas, of my heart.
No tide high enough came to rub them off.
Never thought it would happen.
I now meet a stronger tide that's rubbed them all out
For in you, I see that strength.
Come walk with me in the valley of the lilies,
A symbol of chastity and virtue
Filled with God's love,
Where nothing is impossible.
For all that glitters is not gold.
Come glide with me
On eagles' wings to great heights.
Let us rest in God's own love
For without Him, our souls are forever restless.
Bubbles of love erupt from deep within my heart.
Little vessels of love that travel to where you are.

Strong enough to withstand the elements
to get to where you are—
Wherever you may end up.
I wish you peace, love, and joy,
And my prayer is that you may rest in the love
of Christ Jesus our Lord and Saviour.

Questions

May I dare ask the question?
May I dare think of it?
How do I relate with you?
You were human, yet God.
May I please tell you how I feel inside?
May I truthfully lay my heart on the
table and show you who I am?
My heart is full of feelings,
Bursting at the seams.
I can hold it back no more.
May I dare hold your hand?
May I hug you?
May I step into her shoes,
The shoes of Mary of Magdala?
In my simplicity,
May I come to you?
If I come as I am,
Will you receive me?
Love me?
Understand me?
Or will you reject me?
My Jesus, my Lord will you accept me as broken as I am?

My Three Wishes

My three wishes would be to find love, true love,
a someone I truly connect with deeply.
To grow old and see my children's children, and
To live a life on earth that was worthy enough for
me to Meet my God when I eventually die.
To live and give with generosity.
To treat others with love, be gentle and soft,
Sensitive to others' feelings,
Understanding.
I like a comfortable life.
I work hard for what I need and want.
I don't particularly aspire to be rich, but if God
gives me The wisdom for it, I would be grateful.
I love to share, and if I did accumulate wealth, I
would give a good percentage of it to charity.

Male Companionship

Don't feel like it anymore.
Don't want to anymore.
Do not know why, but I feel it.
I want male companionship not anymore.
I want to be free,
As free as a bird.
Lonesome yet happy, I am full of self-love.
To spend the rest of my life with a man
So distant, so far away, not appealing at all.
Comfortable with my solitude.
I feel better about myself.
I'm pretty and beautiful as I am.
Male companionship for life may whither my delicate soul.
I can feel it coming; I can see it coming
Far across the landscape.
Solitude, lonesomeness, I desperately need.
I have Jesus now.
My life safe in His hands.
My life on earth and in the eternal are safe and secure.
Christ Jesus will see me through.
Male companionship will only ruin the
peace I harbour in my heart.

Male companionship, with its complexities
and his inability to love from the heart—
I don't feel like it anymore.
I don't want to share my delicate soul with anyone.
My soul built for solitude cannot take it anymore.

Life

Life is a passage of time.
Life on earth a dimension,
A battlefield for survival.
Alas, it's a gift.
A struggle to keep your head above the unkind deep waters.
Life is rough.
Life is sweet.
Life is a bed of roses.
Life is like a rail line,
Will only let you pass through a predestined system.
Life is a pain, but the greatest secret to life is endurance.
Life is a road we travel to a destiny we allow.
Life is a paradox; we plan a future we do not own.
For the will of God will always prevail.
Life is a mystery; little bits and pieces
make that much sense.
Be happy and make merry when you can.
Sorrow is but a stone's throw away.
Life is the soul's search for peace, joy, love, and happiness.
However, we search in all the wrong
places but the right ones.

Life is a dream; you will wake up
and find it all gone - death.
Life is what you make it for indeed it's a passage of time, a
Dimension of survival, a paradox, a dream, and a mystery.
Life is a search.
But most of all, life is an extension of
God's love for mankind.
What you make of it is yours to Him.

Death

Without asking, you've taken from me.
With no warning, you tear them from my very arms.
O death, I do despise you
For how dare you?
How dare you take the liberty?
Without asking, you make claim,
A beginning of a new life for them.
They go off to a land a mystery to me.
They say they go to heaven.
Where do souls go when they die, depart their
earthly Tents of a home—their bodies?
Alas, a concept I cannot quite grasp.
My comprehension going only so far.
Death, you are indeed a familiar enemy
For we have too much in common—
the love of my loved ones.
I sit apart in a daze, trying to figure out the mystery.
O death, your sting is like poison to me.

Come, Come

When I thought of Him, I felt His presence.
When I called His name, He was near.
When I looked around, I realised He was part of my life.
Come, come, all you who are weary.
Come, you who are in doubt, in fear, or do
not know what love really means.
You will learn how to share love freely in one spirit.
Jesus is there; He is my refuge,
My strength,
My hope.
He will be yours too if you will Him.
He is ready to come to you.
All you need to do is say, "Yes, Lord."
No price to pay;
One rule to follow:
The rule of love.
When I looked around, I realised He was a part of my life.
Invite Him, and He will be a part of yours.

Lover of My Heart and Soul

All my life, I've been searching.
Are you the man I seek?
Looking, searching, seeking.
Is that you?
Are you Him?
Please tell me.
Is that You,
Lover of my heart and soul,
To touch me like no other?
To heal me like never before?
Are you the one to bring salvation unto my soul?
My Lord my God my Jesus, lover of my very heart and soul.

Time

This time last year, I wished for different, I
aspired for different and I desired different.
Tick tock, tick tock, the moment I laid eyes on
you, my heart melted, and my destiny changed
You brought about a change within me
no other soul has ever done.
Something happened in the cosmos
I am liberated, I am free, I am enlightened.
For I am indeed glad our paths met.
Tick tock, tick tock time passes
The course of my life has changed, forever
This time last year, I yearned for different
My soul was different and my spirit in a different place
Alas! Time, an interesting phenomenon
It heels, it nourishes, it allows acceptance
This time, two years ago, I was a completely
different person to whom I am today.
Tick tock, tick tock time allowed us to meet
Tick tock, tick tock time allows us to move on
Yet in my world, you will always be the
man that I need and adore.

My son

(John-Paul)
A personality that mirrors mine
Seeing my spirit within him
Strong a force to reckon with
A little whirlwind at times
Overflowing with love and affection
A deep thinker, a philosopher
I can only admire his brave little soul
For he has beautifully graced us with
his presence in our lives
I certainly cannot imagine life without him
Reminding me of my own father,
You entered the world the moment my mother departed;
A sadness overshadowing with happiness
Astounding, my little rock
I know you will achieve much
May the hand of the Almighty be upon you always
I love you deeply.

Sunflower

(for my daughter Chileshe)
I call you my sunflower only because you are;
Bright.
Radiant.
Ever so beautiful.
Blessing whomever you meet,
You are a blameless soul, pure and true.
Fragile yet strong.
Small yet powerful.
You kept me alive.
You gave me a reason, purpose, meaning
Together we have been through a lot,
For every day a struggle, I woke up for you
He called you sunshine, only because you are
Bringing happiness to his very soul
He held you in his arms with deep adoration
His love for you unending
He went ever too quickly.
She called you akaliluba kandi (my little flower)
only because you are.
I call you my sunflower, because not only are you
beautiful, you have always been a symbol of
adoration and loyalty standing by my side always.

About the Author

Priscilla was born at the Kings College Hospital (London) to Zambian parents, an electronics engineer and a typist. In the early years of her life, her family returned to Zambia, where she was raised and surrounded by a large extended family alongside her three siblings, of whom she is the youngest.

Adapting to her new settings brought a sense of confusion, uncertainty, and feelings of anxiety because with the "new family", there was stiff competition for parental attention. Feeling the outsider in her own home, she developed a passion for poetry and could escape into her verses and live within her words. Habitually reluctant to share them, she would only show her older brother, who encouraged her. In her teenage years, she would jot a line or two in her friends' scrapbooks.

After studying chemical engineering at the Copperbelt University in Zambia, she returned to England to study at Hertfordshire University and Ulster University. She is currently a biomedical scientist at Luton and Dunstable Hospital NHS Foundation Trust. She lives in Hertfordshire with her husband and two children. Priscilla always had the feeling that one day she should share her poems with the world. The time is now.

Lightning Source UK Ltd.
Milton Keynes UK
UKHW010617210719
346476UK00001B/66/P